Belgium and
Luxembourg

Editors Lesley Firth
             Dale Gunthorp
Design Patrick Frean
Picture Research Mary Walsh
Production Rosemary Bishop
             Vivienne Driscoll
Illustrations Hayward Associates
             Patrick Frean
             Tony Payne
             John Shackell
Maps Matthews and Taylor Associates
Consultant Frank E. Huggett

First published 1976
Macdonald Educational Ltd.
Holywell House, Worship Street,
London E.C.2.

© Macdonald Educational Ltd. 1976

ISBN 0-382-06118-7

Published in the United
States by Silver Burdett
Company, Morristown, N. J.
1977 Printing

Library of Congress
Catalog Card No. 77-70194

The cover shows the flower market in the
Grand' Place, Brussels.

The endpaper shows Viandey Castle in
Luxembourg.

Page 6 shows a street scene in Bruges,
Belgium.

Belgium and Luxembourg

the lands and their people

Joan and George Morey

Macdonald Educational

Contents

Belgium's golden age

A divided nation

The kingdom of Belgium came into being in 1831, but the region that we now know as Belgium has a long, interesting history going back to Roman times.

Belgium is a country with no natural frontiers, apart from a short coastline. It has three official languages: French, Dutch and German. Its biggest problem is that the country is divided between the Flemings, who speak Dutch, and the Walloons, who speak French.

In recent years the differences between these two groups have developed into public quarrels. Despite their differences, the Belgians have a sense of national unity. For example, the Flemings and Walloons will join together to support the Belgian football team in international matches, and everyone was delighted when the Belgian cyclist Eddy Merckx won the Tour de France!

◀ Charlemagne (742-814 A.D.), first Holy Roman Emperor. He was one of the founders of Western civilization after the fall of Rome. Belgium was part of his empire, which covered a large area of Europe.

▼ The Cloth Hall, Ypres. The original building was built in the Middle Ages when Ypres was important for the trade in woollen cloth. The Cloth Hall was destroyed in World War I. It has been rebuilt to look like the original building.

The Middle Ages

In the past, Belgium has often been fought over and divided by foreign armies. The Belgians were sometimes able to turn the position to their advantage. In the Middle Ages, towns such as Ypres, Ghent and Bruges won wealth and fame as centres of trade and industry although Belgium was ruled by foreign overlords.

Belgium's great days lasted only from the twelfth until the early fifteenth century. During that time, many fine buildings were erected and the Flemish school of painting flourished.

Decline began as rival nations rose in power. The decline became rapid when the Dutch rebelled against the Spaniards, who then ruled the Low Countries. The Belgians joined in revolt against the Spaniards, but were defeated and severely punished. It was not until the nineteenth century that Belgium began to thrive again.

▲ *Peasants Dancing* by Pieter Brueghel the Elder (c. 1525-69). Many of his paintings have survived, and give a brilliant idea of how ordinary Flemish people lived in the 16th century. The picture shows peasants enjoying one of the many religious holidays.

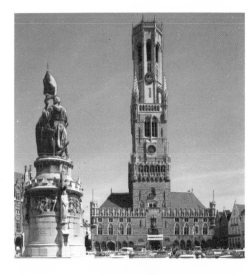

◄ Philip the Good, Duke of Burgundy (1419-67) hearing Mass. He did much to encourage the arts in the Low Countries.

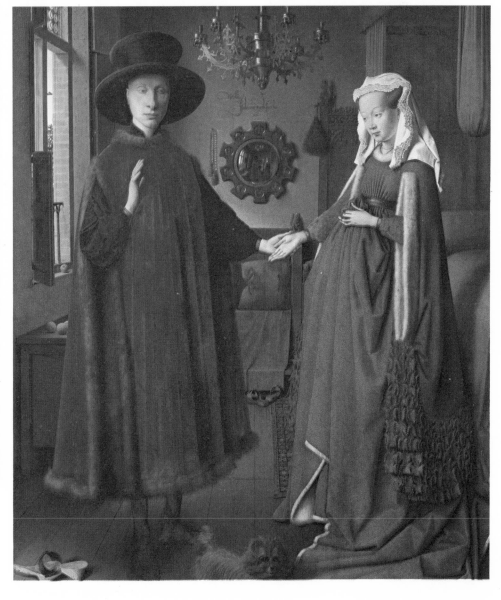

▶ *Giovanni Arnolfini and his wife* by Jan van Eyck (c. 1390-41). This gives a good idea of how the interior of a rich Flemish house looked. The Belgian cities were so important at that time that many Italian merchants lived there.

The land of Belgium

Varied scenery

Belgium is a small country. It is not much bigger than Wales or Maryland. The boundaries are never further than 322 km. (200 miles) apart. Belgium is also one of the most thickly populated countries in Europe, so that in many parts of the country one is never very far from a house. The motorist, who dashes across Belgium on his way elsewhere, sees the least interesting part of the country and misses a great deal.

For so small a country, the scenery is very varied. In the north-west, the dykes and polders which protect the land from the sea, and the canals and watercourses which drain the low-lying fields, recall the landscape of the Netherlands. The highest ground, and the most thickly wooded areas, are to be found in the Ardennes, which include much of southern Belgium.

Belgium is not naturally a rich and fertile land. Its climate is colder and damper than that of the British Isles. It is said to rain on more than 200 days a year. The hard work of generations of peasants has made the land productive.

North of the French border, the district around Mons and Charleroi serves as a reminder that Belgium is a highly industrialised country. This is only one of a number of industrial centres. The surroundings are scarcely different from what is to be seen in northern France.

Flanders

The scenery quickly changes as one moves into Flanders. The Flemish houses are often built of red brick and have high-pitched roofs. They have iron roller-shutters at the windows which, when lowered, often give the odd impression that the village is deserted!

A curious thing is that the houses, often designed to stand in terraced rows along a street, are instead built in ones and twos. This gives the owners more privacy, but it adds greatly to the cost of the house. It is not necessary to go far in Flanders before seeing some of the new factories, many foreign-owned, which are bringing prosperity.

A country of contrasts

Boating and bathing on the coast

Market place at Antwerp

Grand'Place at Brussels

Knokke

Bruges

Antwerp

Ghent

Brussels

Scheldt

Carnival of the Blancs Moussis at Stavelot

Canals and windmills in Flanders

Mons

Namur

Meuse

Liège

Meuse Valley

Ardennes

Coal-mining and iron foundries in the Mons region

Horse-riding in the Ardennes

LUXEM-BOURG

Château Jehay in the Meuse Valley

▼ One of the many beautiful canals in Bruges. A trip by motor boat offers an excellent way of seeing the fine old houses. Bruges gets its name from the many bridges which cross the canals.

▲ Farmland in the Ardennes. Some of the best cattle-raising country is found where forest land has been cleared. Belgium's white-blue and red-white cattle deserve to be better known abroad.

▼ Brussels by night. The Grand' Place, at the centre of the oldest part of Brussels, is floodlit at night. The 17th century houses around the square are dominated by the belfry of the Town Hall.

▲ The Freyr Rocks, near Dinant. The valley of the Meuse south of Dinant has some of the most attractive scenery in Belgium. The limestone hills on its right bank dominate a gently flowing river which attracts many visitors during the summer.

Luxembourg and its people

An important place in history

The Grand Duchy of Luxembourg is smaller than Cornwall or Rhode Island. With such powerful neighbours as France, Germany and Belgium, it is surprising that Luxembourg survived in times past, but it has an independent ruler, and the people speak a dialect of their own.

Luxembourg has had an important place in history. Four of its rulers became emperors of the Holy Roman Empire. The end of Luxembourg seemed to be near in the last century. In 1815, it was given to the Dutch King. Then, in 1831, after Belgium had revolted against the Dutch, the Belgians acquired a large part of Luxembourg, which they have kept as the county of Luxembourg. The Germans and French, too, were always anxious to acquire the land.

Wine and steel

Luxembourg is a beautiful country. The northern half is wooded and hilly; the southern is fine agricultural land and produces wine. On the extreme southern edge is a small, but very important industrial area, producing a great deal of steel. Luxembourg industry is important today because of the work of a Briton, Sidney Gilchrist Thomas. Luxembourg has a lot of iron ore, but it was useless for steelmaking because it contained phosphorous. Gilchrist Thomas found a way to remove the impurities, and a great industry was born, which ensures the Luxembourgers a very high standard of living.

European unity

Luxembourg is very proud to have shown Europe the way to unity. In 1921, it entered into a customs union with Belgium. After World War II the Netherlands was included, to form Benelux. Luxembourg was one of the founder members of the Common Market. The European Court meets in Luxembourg, and some of the departments of the Common Market have their offices there.

The changing boundaries of Luxembourg

St. Vith
Marche
St. Hubert
Bitburg
Orchimont
Grand Duchy of Luxembourg
Arlon
Luxembourg
Virton
Montmédy
Marville
Thionville

Present-day Luxembourg
Territory ceded to Belgium in 1839
Territory ceded to Prussia in 1815
Territory ceded to France in 1659

▲ Luxembourg's changing boundaries. Her lands have often been sought by neighbours. The biggest change occurred after 1831, when a large area was given to Belgium.

▼ H.R.H. the Grand Duke Jean of Luxembourg with his family. The Grand Duke succeeded in 1964, when his mother abdicated after reigning for 45 years.

▲ Luxembourg City. Part of the city has been built around steep river gorges. The city has 93 bridges, the biggest being the Grand Duchess Charlotte Bridge.

► A cafe scene in Luxembourg City. The city enjoys a warmer and drier climate than much of neighbouring Belgium. It is often possible in summer to spend an hour with friends in an open air cafe.

▲ Clervaux Castle. The old turreted castle was built in the 16th century by the powerful Counts of Lannoi. It was severely damaged in 1944, but has been restored.

► An iron foundry in southern Luxembourg. Luxembourg owes much of its prosperity to steel. In 1973, it produced nearly 6 million tons of crude steel.

Family life

Belgian families and the law

Many Belgians, like the French, keep their home life private. You would probably have to know a Belgian family for a long time before being invited to spend an evening in their home. Even close friends often prefer to entertain one another in a restaurant. Attitudes are changing, but old ideas still persist.

Within the home, family ties are strong, and the law makes them stronger still. It is not unusual to find the old grandmother occupying part of a house, while her son and his family occupy the rest. This is not entirely a matter of kindness. The law gives her the right to a share of the old home.

Many of the older terraced Belgian houses are surprisingly narrow, and this often means that a house is three rooms deep. The owners get over the problem of lighting the room in the middle, without windows, by a skilful use of mirrors. The reason for this narrowness is that the householder is responsible for the pavement outside the house. If a passerby injures himself because the pavement is not properly kept, the householder is held responsible, and so he keeps his frontage as narrow as possible.

Now that so many foreigners live in Belgium, foreign ideas of house building are becoming better known. It is increasingly common in the more expensive suburbs to find bungalow-type houses with flat roofs, and fine front gardens.

Inside the home

For many people, the Belgian living room in winter would be much too hot, for the big radiators would be fully on. The Belgians have a morbid fear of "a current of air" and even in summer windows are likely to be closed, and the curtains drawn.

Everyone is impressed by the number of houseplants to be found even in the poorest houses, and also by the cleanliness and good order. The tiled floors of the older houses make it easy to take a bucket and mop and wash the rooms right through.

The journey homewards from work begins about 4.30 p.m. This leaves a long evening, which the family often spends together.

▼ A Luxembourg farming family eats lunch in the fields. When the weather is fine, the farmer spends every possible moment working. When they are on holiday from school the children lend a hand.

A working class family budget

Food consumed at home — 24·7%

Tobacco and drink consumed at home 4·5%

Shoes and clothing — 10·7%

Rent, rates, electricity, gas and other fuels — 18·7%

Household durable articles — 9·3%

Private cars and public transport — 11·4%

Entertainment, restaurants, cafés — 9·9%

Other expenses — 10·8%

Bulletin de statistique, Brussels 1975

▲ Manual workers in Belgium spend proportionately much more than office workers and managers on food and drink, and less rent and entertainment. Food and rent take nearly half a pensioner's income.

▶ A Belgian family at table in their Brussels flat. Many Belgian families have their main meal at mid-day, if they are able to travel home.

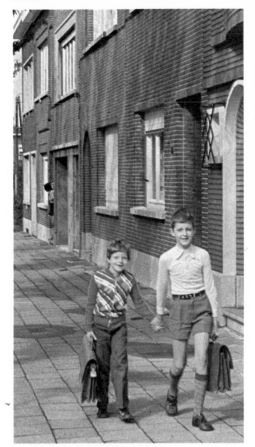

◀ The Brussels street in which the family lives. Many Belgians prefer houses to flats. It is easier to find a home to live in than in most other countries.

▼ The family relaxes together in the evening. This family is wealthier than many Belgian families, and is able to afford a very comfortable home.

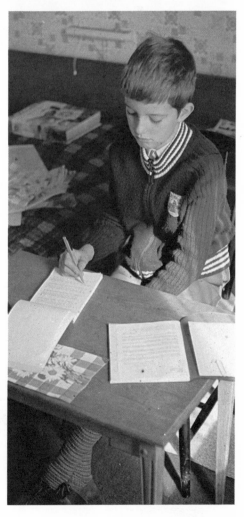

▲ The young son of the family doing his homework. He is fortunate in having a place of his own in which to work undisturbed. Most parents are interested to see that homework is well done.

15

Leisure and pleasure

Increased leisure time

The Belgians have a reputation for hard work, relieved only at intervals by bouts of noisy, exuberant fun. In fact, people in paid jobs have benefited by reduced hours, so that a forty-hour week is common for many workers.

There is nothing to prevent a person from taking a second job in his leisure time. However, for many workers, it means more time for their racing pigeons, rabbits and plants, or for a quiet drink and talk with their friends. The high cost of labour has also meant that the "do-it-yourself" movement has made big strides in Belgium.

Young Belgians often make use of their free time by riding around the countryside on their cycles, and going to the cinema, or on organised trips. Many take part in events arranged locally by young people.

Wealthier Belgians use their cars for trips into the countryside, or for visiting relations. They see their leisure time also as an opportunity to read or study, to talk to friends, as well as to watch television.

For many Belgians, Friday evening, out of season, is the signal to pack the car for a weekend at a hotel on the coast, where they will find sumptuous meals and have an opportunity to gamble at the local casino.

▼ Belgium, like many European countries, has a State lottery, with prizes every month. Many people find the hope of sudden riches hard to resist, especially as the draw approaches.

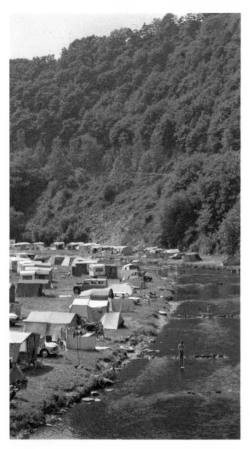

▲ A camp site on the River Sûre, Luxembourg. There are many similar sites in rural holiday areas. Campers often spend a great deal on their equipment, and insist that the camp is kept in very good order.

► Cafes on the Grand' Place, Brussels. These attract thousands of visitors, who enjoy the finest scene in old Brussels. During the week, the flower market in the square makes a colourful scene, and on Sundays there is a bird market. Belgians usually leave these cafes to the tourists.

▲ The casinos at some of the more famous holiday centres such as Spa, Ostend and Knokke, attract many visitors. In winter, some Belgians include a visit to the gaming tables in a weekend's relaxation.

▲ A sailing lesson for young people in Ostend harbour. When the beginners know how to manage the sails, the boat is taken out into the sea. In calm weather this is an ideal place to learn.

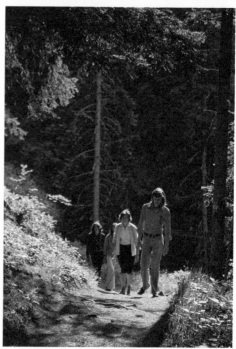

▲ Hikers walking in the Ardennes. The region offers some of the finest walking country in Europe. The hills are not very high, but it is possible to get wonderful views over the surrounding countryside. At every holiday centre there is a fine choice of walks.

◄ The seashore at Blankenberge. Blankenberge has grown from a small fishing village into one of the most important seaside resorts in Belgium. Its special attraction is the long, sandy beach. At low tide, it is wide and safe for bathing.

A variety of sports

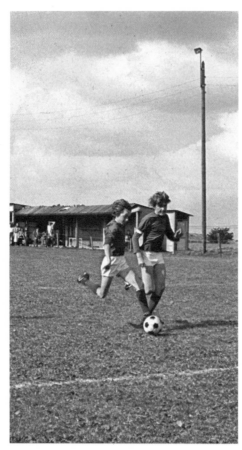

▶ Football is a very popular sport in Belgium, and there are hundreds of clubs. People watch the fortunes of foreign clubs closely, and if a Belgian club beats one of them the excitement is great.

Armchair sportsmen

Many Belgians are keenly interested in sport, but most of them prefer to read about it, or watch it, rather than take part themselves. A recent survey showed that, on average, a Belgian spent only 6 minutes a day at sport. Since this figure included professionals and young men and women, it means that many spent no time at all at sport.

A good football match, or a local cycle race, will always draw a crowd of spectators, since these are the favourite sports. But the average Belgian, who is probably tired at the end of the week, and not always sure when he will be free, often likes to take part in sports which call for little organization.

Belgium's many fine rivers provide excellent sport and the best spots are often lined with keen fishermen. The Belgians have borrowed the game of *petanche* from the French. This game can be played in a quiet

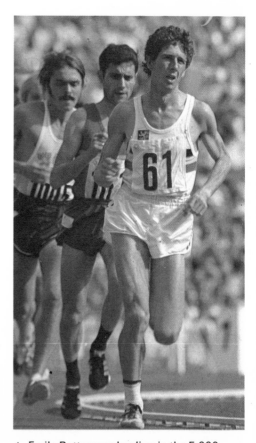

▲ Emile Puttemans leading in the 5,000 metres event at the Munich Olympic Games. Although he was unplaced then, he set up a world record of 13 min. 13 sec. for the same distance during 1972.

◀ Eddy Merckx wins the final sprint in the Swiss professional championship. In his ten years as a professional, he has won 385 victories, and won the Tour de France five times in six years.

corner such as the town square. It is a form of bowls, played with heavy metal balls, slightly bigger than cricket balls. *Pelote*, too, which is a mixture of tennis and handball, can be played in streets and squares.

Cycling

Belgium offers everything from tennis and horse racing to sand yachting, but the sport which excites every young Belgian is cycling. Belgians have recently done exceptionally well in international competitions, and every boy dreams of winning the Tour de France, and beating the best riders of France, Italy and Spain.

Belgium has never tried to win international honours by spending great sums of State money in training athletes, as some countries have done. Even its soccer players are not full-timers. They have their own jobs during the week, and are paid match-money when they appear for their club.

▶ Pigeons being released from baskets at the start of a race. The pigeons are sent by rail to a distant starting place, the first one home being the winner. A good racing pigeon is worth a lot of money.

▲ Jackie Ickx, Belgium's most famous racing driver. He has distinguished himself in sports car and Formula 1 racing on many of the world's circuits as a driver for Ferrari, Matra and Brabham-Ford.

▶ A race on the Francorchamps circuit. Francorchamps is Belgium's most important race track. Like Le Mans, it makes use of public main roads in places. It is 14 km. (8 miles) in circuit.

Francorchamps racetrack

La Source
Pits
Quarry
Blanchimont
Eau Rouge
Cottage
Haut de la Cote
Stavelot
Masta
Burnenville
Malmédy

Tradition in education

Church and State schools

Many Belgian children start going to school at the age of two or three years, but they do not have formal lessons, and school is not compulsory until the age of six.

Parents can choose whether to send their children to a Church school or to a State school. The cost of maintaining both types of school is met by the State, and both are organized on similar lines. In most Catholic schools, boys and girls are taught separately. There are as yet few comprehensive schools.

The primary schools have a five-day week, with Wednesday afternoons free. The secondary schools may choose between a five-day week, or a six-day week with Wednesday and Saturday afternoons off. Teaching is carried out in the language of the district.

Discipline and formality

The educational system of Belgium is in the process of being reshaped. In the meantime, a foreign visitor may well feel that education is formal, and discipline strict. There is little place for sport. The best equipped school have gymnasiums, but one is unlikely to find Belgian schools surrounded with acres of playing fields. Many schools are old-fashioned by modern standards, and may, at best, have an asphalt playground. Very often, because space is hard to find, or perhaps because of the "population bulge", schools are tucked away in unlikely buildings.

The Belgian school system

Nursery schools — 3-6 years

12-15 years — Ecoles moyennes and schools giving technical and vocational tuition

15-18 years — Primary teacher training — Tech. and vocational training

18 years and over — Art and architecture — Advanced tech. education

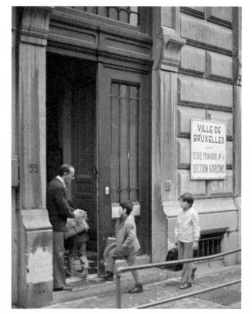

▲ The beginning of another day at school. School buildings in Belgium often lack space for recreation. Frequent school trips to places of interest make up for lack of opportunity to play.

▶ A Belgian classroom. This is a school for girls only. Although big reforms in education are taking place, Belgian teaching methods are traditional, and discipline is strict.

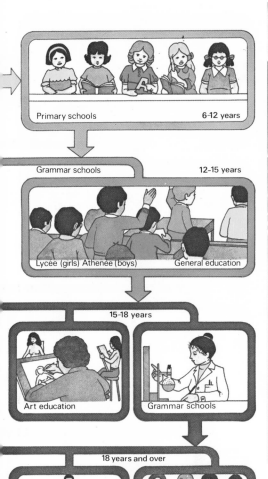

Primary schools — 6-12 years

Grammar schools — 12-15 years

Lycee (girls) Athenee (boys) — General education

15-18 years

Art education

Grammar schools

18 years and over

Higher teacher training

University

▲ The gymnasium at the European School, Brussels. The school is intended for the children of Common Market officials, but others may join if places are available. Children are taught in their native language, plus one other E.E.C. language.

▼ Pupils in the science laboratory of a Belgian school. Generally, Belgian schools are less well equipped than they might be, because of the cost of satisfying differing requirements of Church and State schools, and Flemings and Walloons.

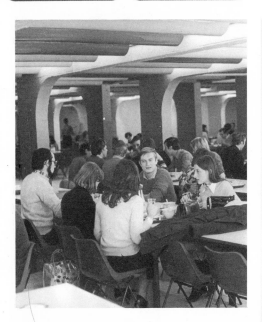

▲ The University canteen at Louvain-le-Neuve. After the language riots in the 1960s, the French faculties of Louvain University moved out to a new site at Ottignies.

Customs and carnivals

Keeping ancient customs alive

The Belgians love carnivals and processions, and enter into the spirit of the occasion with great enthusiasm. These festivities make a welcome break from hard work, and are occasions for family reunions.

The simplest processions, with flower-decorated cars and floats, interspersed with bands and parades of boys and girls in uniform, cost a great deal of money. Many of the events are far more elaborate. Although Belgium only became a kingdom in 1831, it has a long history and many events celebrate some important occasion in a town's history, or serve as a reminder of an ancient custom.

Some customs are so old that their origins are forgotten, and these must go back to pagan times. There are many tree legends. The Cracknel Festival at Geraardsbergen ends at nightfall with the ceremonial burning of a tree—a signal for the lighting of bonfires in the countryside around. However, it is hard to find a reason why, earlier in the day, the burgomaster and aldermen climb a little hill outside the town to drink a toast from a goblet of wine in which tiny fish are swimming around!

Religious origins

Some of the most important celebrations are religious in origin. One of the most important is the Procession of the Holy Blood at Bruges, when a crystal phial, said to contains drops of Christ's blood, is taken in procession.

A strange, but moving, spectacle is the Procession of the Penitents in the little town of Veurne, where people carry heavy crosses through the streets. The monks' robes which they wear, and the cowls over their heads, are very Spanish in character, and are a reminder that the Spaniards ruled Flanders for a long time.

Some people say that the carnivals are not what they were: that the motorcar has made it possible for people to meet together often and that people are becoming too sophisticated. But the carnivals continue to attract thousands.

▲ A guild festival in the Campine. The leaders wear the insignia of their office. Such festivals make a pleasant break from routine in remote country districts.

◄ The Shrove Tuesday Festival of the Gilles at Binche. During the procession, the Gilles, in their magnificent costumes, throw oranges to the crowd.

▼ Veurne: the Procession of the Penitents. This is held on the last Sunday in July. It is a reminder of the Spanish occupation, when Veurne was an important town.

Some famous Belgian festivals

▲ Ath: Procession of the Giants. The wedding of the giant, Goliath, takes place on the last Saturday in August. This is followed next day by a procession when the wicker-work giants "dance" through the streets.

▲ Fosse-la-Ville: In the mid-Lent carnival, the Chinels, whose costume reminds one of Mr. Punch's, dance through the street.

▲ Ostend: Blessing of the Sea. All the ships are beflagged, and sound their sirens in response to the Blessing.

▲ St. Severin-en-Condroz: Christmas Nativity Play. The play takes place in the village church, and village children take part.

▲ Bruges: Procession of the Holy Blood. On Ascension Day, the return of the Crusaders with their Holy Relic is re-enacted.

▲ Geraardsbergen: the Cracknel Festival is held on the last Sunday in February, on a small hill outside the town.

▲ Mons: Battle of the Lumeçon. At the end of the procession, St. George takes up the fight with the dragon, the Lumecon.

▲ Ypres: Procession of the Cats. During the procession, replicas of cats and witches are thrown to the crowd.

Patronage in the arts

Flemish art

Between the time of Jan van Eyck and Paul Rubens, the Flemish School produced some of the world's greatest art. At the same time Flemish architects were designing buildings of lasting beauty. The Low Countries were fortunate in producing artists of genius at a time when there were rich citizens who could support them with commissions.

The arts today

In modern Belgium, the place of the rich merchant has been taken over by business firms and the State. The Banque Lambert has one of the best collections of modern art in Belgium. The State, for example, by subsidizing Jeunesse Musicale and the Queen Elizabeth International Musical Contest, has done much to promote musical studies.

In music and the theatre, finances are more difficult. The opportunity to earn bigger fees in Paris and Amsterdam has attracted the best Belgian talent.

People who would like to do something for the theatre have been faced with three problems: general indifference on the part of the public, the language problem, and the readiness of Belgians to take, at second-hand, what has been produced abroad.

In these circumstances, the work at the Opéra de la Monnaie in Brussels, of Maurice Béjart and his ballet company, and of young groups like Internationale Nieuwe Scene, is a great achievement.

▲ *Christ, St. John, an angel and a little girl,* by Paul Rubens (1577-1640). Rubens was greatly influenced by his years of study in Italy, and became one of the greatest painters of his age. His fine house in Antwerp became a meeting place for many distinguished people. It is now a museum.

▲ *Self Portrait* by James Ensor (1860-1949). Ensor was an Englishman, who later became a naturalized Belgian. His paintings of grotesque masks and animated skeletons, and his other Expressionist works, had a great influence upon other Belgian artists.

▶ A scene from *The Ballad of the Big and Small Puppets* presented by the young Antwerp theatre company, Internationale Nieuwe Scene. Their lively presentations have won praise even from critics who do not always approve of the social message of their plays.

▲ A scene from Maurice Béjart's presentation of Stravinsky's *Firebird*. Although Béjart is a Frenchman, he works in Brussels, and has given his group an international reputation.

► César Franck (1822-90) was Belgium's greatest musician. His many works include Symphonic Variations for piano and orchestra. He worked mainly in Paris.

◄ Detail from *La Méditation* by René Magritte (1898-1967). Like many Belgian painters, Magritte was a surrealist.

▼ *The Conjurer* by Hieronymus Bosch (1480-1516). A group of peasants watches as a conjurer does the thimble trick. Much of Bosch's work is symbolic.

Shops and markets

Small shops

The small shopkeeper has an important place in Belgian life. Such businesses are often open for long hours, and sell things which nobody else would bother to stock.

Such shopkeepers have not had an easy time. In 1975, they called a one-day strike when the Government pegged prices. A few years ago they were ordered to close for at least one day each week, and for two weeks in the summer. At the same time, the law restricting the growth of big multiple shops was repealed.

Some of the small grocers have been able to help themselves by introducing self-service, and by forming into groups, which can take advantage of bulk buying. The small delicatessens continue to flourish. It makes one hungry to look at the prepared food in the windows!

One type of shop which seems to have escaped the move to modernization is the chemist's. Some shops, even in the centre of Brussels, do not seem to have changed in a hundred years. One half expects the chemist to grind up some powders and make some pills on the spot instead of producing modern manufactured medicines.

Markets and supermarkets

The many open air markets, to be found in streets and squares of many towns, are a feature of Belgian life. Some of the best and freshest fruit and vegetables can be bought there. However, the big stores and supermarkets continue to grow. Often there is a giant store on the edge of town, with room for many cars. The shopping centre at Woluwe even has a church among its facilities.

▼ A shop selling prepared game birds. Such shops are also likely to sell the delightful meat patés, of which there are several varieties. Belgian food shops maintain very high standards.

▲ A lace shop in Bruges. In summer, many old ladies sit at their doors enjoying the sun as they make their lace. It is fascinating to watch as they move the bobbins about to produce the patterns.

◄ A Brussels "flea market". The most famous of these is in the Place du Jeu de Balle, in Les Marolles quarter, and is open every morning. Here one is likely to find anything: clothes, ornaments, books, antiques, and sometimes a bargain. Whether one buys or not, the flea market is always interesting.

▲ One of the many fine vegetable markets in Brussels. Housewives find the journey worthwhile because the produce is usually fresh and fairly cheap.

◄ Some Belgian currency. This money can be used in Belgium and Luxembourg, although Luxembourg money is not readily accepted in Belgium. Coins are issued for values of 10 francs down to $\frac{1}{4}$ franc.

▲ A check-out point in a Belgian supermarket. Supermarkets are to be found in all the larger towns. The notice in Flemish (above) asks customers to help the cashier by having their money ready.

◄ The Galeries St. Hubert in Brussels. This is the most beautiful of all the Brussels arcades, and the oldest in Europe. It is lined by fine shops. Since the weather in Brussels often discourages window-shopping, many of the new buildings have shopping arcades.

Eating the Belgian way

Belgian restaurants

Most Belgians delight in good food. They are prepared to spend a lot of money on a good meal, and in return expect generous helpings. Brussels has many restaurants. In some of the old streets, such as the Rue des Bouchers, the restaurants often stand side by side on both sides of the street.

Although rising costs limit the opportunities for eating out, the best restaurants continue to flourish. They are seldom very big, and in summer chairs and tables are sometimes set out in the middle of the street for late-comers. Away from the centre of Brussels, some good restaurants are in private houses, where the family has given over its best rooms as a restaurant.

Belgian cooking

Belgian cooking relies heavily upon dishes which the French have made famous. Occasionally, famous French chefs are invited by Belgian hotels to arrange a *weekend gastronomique*, but generally one would have to travel a long way to find Belgian restaurants which equal the best of the French. Belgians who can afford the cost take weekend trips to eat in Paris restaurants.

Belgium has fine dishes of its own. Its seafood is outstanding. Mussels are eaten in huge quantities. They are often served hot in a savoury broth, and eaten with mustard. The waiter will pretend to be disappointed if you do not finish two big platefuls! Another famous dish is *waterzooi*, made of a variety of fish served in a broth. Chicken is often used instead.

Nearly every region has its specialities, such as *porc à la St. Hubert* from the Ardennes, which is especially good if wild boar meat is used, and *anguilles à la vert*—"green eels", a speciality of Antwerp.

Belgians drink a lot of beer. Much of it is of a lager type and is imported. One traditional Belgian beer is called *gueuze*. Another interesting beer is *kriek*, which is flavoured with cherries.

Belgian seafood

▲ Oysters are a favourite dish, but they are rather expensive. Many are reared in the quiet backwaters of Zeeland.

▲ The Belgians have created many delicious fish soups. *Waterzooi* includes both fresh and salt water fish.

▲ Mussels are popular. One way of serving them is to grill them with breadcrumbs and grated cheese.

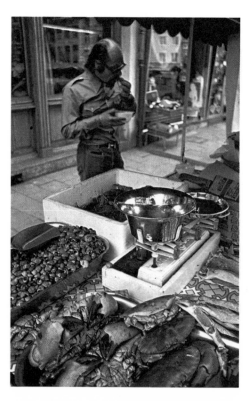

▲ A seafood stall. There are many such stalls in market places. This stall sells various kinds of shell fish, such as crabs, winkles and whelks. These can be eaten on the spot or taken home.

Make yourself a Belgian meal

ENDIVE WITH HAM

2 lb endive (chicory) heads
8 slices boiled ham
juice of 1 lemon
4 oz Gruyère cheese, grated
pinch of salt
water
white sauce

Wash and trim the endive heads. Put them into a saucepan with the lemon juice, salt and water. Boil for 15 minutes. In the meantime, make a white sauce as follows. Melt a knob of butter in a heavy pan and add enough plain flour to make a stiff paste. Gradually add milk to the paste, stirring constantly so that it thickens into a smooth white sauce. Season the sauce with salt and pepper. When the endive is cooked, drain it and press out excess water. Roll each endive head in a slice of ham and place it in a shallow oven-proof dish. Cover the endive and ham with the white sauce and sprinkle with grated cheese. Bake it in a moderate oven (Gas 4, Electricity 350°F) for 10 minutes.

◄ Fishing for shrimps on the Belgian coast. Fishermen ride horses, dragging the heavy nets, through the shallow waters.

▼ An evening meal in a popular Brussels restaurant. Nearly everyone has ordered mussels. Prices are high, but the best restaurants are very busy.

CARBONNADE OF BEEF

1½ lbs stewing or braising steak
1 lb onions, chopped
salt and pepper
4 oz butter or lard
½ pint beef stock
½ pint beer
1 oz plain flour
1 tablespoon brown sugar

Trim any fat off the meat and cut it into chunks. Season with salt and pepper. Melt the butter or lard in a frying pan and brown the meat in it quickly. Remove the meat from the pan. Add the chopped onions to the frying pan and cook until soft. Place the meat and onions in layers in a heavy stew-pan. Add the beer and some of the beef stock. Stir the flour into the fat remaining in the frying pan and add the rest of the beef stock slowly so that it thickens. Add the thickened stock to the meat and onions in the stew-pan and season with the sugar. Cover the pan and cook gently for two hours. Serve with boiled potatoes and vegetables.

WHITE CHEESECAKE

6 oz flaky pastry
1 lb unsalted curd cheese
2 oz castor sugar
pinch of salt
1 oz flour
2 egg yolks
2 tablespoons softened butter
2 egg whites
sugar for glazing

Line a shallow eight-inch flan ring or pie dish with the pastry. Crumble the cheese into a large bowl and add the castor sugar, salt, flour, egg yolks and butter. Mix these together thoroughly. Whip the egg whites and gently fold them into the mixture. Fill the pastry case with the mixture. Bake in a hot oven (Gas 7, Electricity 425°F) for about 25 minutes, until the cheesecake is firm. Sprinkle the top of the cheesecake with sugar and raise the temperature of the oven (Gas 8, Electricity 450°F) for a few minutes to glaze the top.

▲ Gathering endives. Endives are exported all over Europe, where they are used in salads. Belgians originally grew chicory (endives) to mix the roots with coffee, and then found that the shoots were nice to eat.

29

Creating a kingdom

▲ Waterloo, the Battle of Mont St. Jean, June 1815. The battle resulted in the final defeat of Napoleon. Until the last hour it was not certain that the British and their allies would be victorious.

Belgian independence

After Napoleon had been defeated at Waterloo in 1815, it was felt that France should be prevented from threatening Europe again. Britain wished to prevent France from ever again winning control of Antwerp and the River Scheldt.

A Kingdom of the Netherlands which included Belgium was therefore created, with a Dutchman, Prince William, as King. The arrangement did not please the Belgians, who began to complain that they were being exploited. In 1830, they rebelled, and declared themselves independent. They were supported by Britain, and in 1831, Leopold of Saxe-Coburg was invited to become the first King of the Belgians.

The Dutch, at first, refused to recognise the new State, and nobody thought that it could last long. It seemed impossible to make a nation of two groups as different as the Walloons and the Flemings. The new country had only one natural frontier, and her neighbours seemed to be waiting for a chance to swallow her.

Belgium survived largely because of Leopold's diplomatic skill and the support which Britain gave. He began, in 1831, by persuading the Belgians to accept a very harsh treaty, when nothing better could be had. He understood that Belgium needed to become stable and economically strong. He was even ready to defy the British, at the time of the Crimean War, to maintain the principle that Belgium must remain neutral at all times. When Leopold died in 1865 the survival of Belgium was assured.

► A statue of William II, King of the Netherlands (1840-49) in Luxembourg. Luxembourg remained the private possession of the Dutch Crown until 1890, when the present ruling family succeeded.

▼ Belgian insurgents attack Dutch troops in the Royal Park, Brussels, September 1830. This brought an end to the revolution, and the Dutch troops withdrew from the capital.

Leopold II

His successor, Leopold II (1865–1909) was welcomed to the throne as the first truly Belgian king. The nation at that time was involved in a great industrial and agricultural revolution. Leopold's ambition was to have a share in the development of Africa. In spite of opposition, he proceeded to acquire the Congo. Judged by the standards of the time, it was a brilliant stroke of business and diplomacy. It helped to make Belgium a rich and important nation.

► Leopold I taking the oath as King of the Belgians in July 1831. Leopold, who had been a German prince before accepting the throne, was uncle of the future Queen Victoria of Britain.

▼ *Strike Evening,* a painting by Eugene Laermans. Belgian workers suffered great hardships during the industrial revolution of the 19th century, and this led to many strikes and lock-outs.

▼ Leopold II (1865-1909). In his reign, Belgium became a rich and important country, largely by developing the resources of the Congo. In spite of the ambitions of the other great Powers, he was able to ensure that Belgium enjoyed a long period of peace.

Belgium as a battleground

The First World War

The neutrality of Belgium had been guaranteed. However, it was well-known that Germany was considering the possibility of bypassing the French defences, in the event of war, by invading Belgium. On August 4th, 1914, German troops crossed into Belgium, and the world watched aghast as the new German guns crushed the Belgian defences.

Nearly all of Belgium was quickly overrun. The Belgians flooded the Germans out of trenches near the River Yser, and thus prevented them from capturing the last corner of Belgium. King Albert (1909–34) and his army remained to fight the Germans until the end of the war. Belgium suffered severely before the Germans were defeated in 1918.

The Second World War

War threatened again in 1939. In Belgium, disagreements prevented the planning of proper defences. When, therefore, Hitler invaded Belgium on May 10th, 1940, he found little to halt his drive. On May 28th, King Leopold of the Belgians surrendered, and it was left to the Belgian government and a few brave people to escape and continue the struggle.

The invasion of Belgium, 1914

German advances

▲ The German advance through Belgium in World War I. Their intention to move quickly towards Paris was frustrated. Some of the heaviest battles were fought in Belgium.

▶ King Albert I (1909-34). By refusing to surrender, or to leave Belgium, Albert emerged as his country's hero.

▼ Belgian infantry moving up to the front during World War I. Although they could not hope to win, the Belgians managed to hold onto a small corner of their country.

▲ A war cemetery in Passchendaele. Around Ypres there are many cemeteries where soldiers of World War I are buried.

◄ British troops hauling a gun out of the mud in August 1917. Shell-fire destroyed the drainage system and made conditions terrible.

▼ German troops removing barricades after the surrender of Brussels, May 17th, 1940. The ease with which Belgium was conquered convinced the Germans that the war would be won quickly.

▲ The magazine *Punch* published this famous cartoon in which the Kaiser taunts King Albert with having lost everything. "But not my soul!" the King proudly replies.

Antwerp, a great port

The history of Antwerp

Although Antwerp lies 88 km. (55 miles) from the sea, on the banks of the River Scheldt, it is one of the greatest ports of Europe. In the Middle Ages, while Bruges flourished, Antwerp was no more than a river port. The storms which blocked up the entrance to Bruges, opened up the Scheldt to shipping.

This was very welcome to foreign merchants. They had always been more free to trade in Antwerp than they had been in Bruges. The time was also favourable. Neither France nor the Netherlands had the ports to handle the trade which was arriving from the Far East and the West Indies. By the beginning of the sixteenth century, Antwerp had a thousand foreign businesses dealing with Italy, Spain, and the rest of Europe. People could well say, "Antwerp owes the Scheldt to God, and everything else to the Scheldt".

This early prosperity did not last long. The Dutch rose in revolt against the Spanish overlords, and closed the Scheldt. When the people of Antwerp tried to follow their example, the revolt was severely crushed. For many years after, the Dutch maintained their stranglehold on Antwerp, and demanded heavy tolls from ships using the port.

Antwerp today

Since the Second World War, Antwerp has undergone great development. New factories have sprung up, and the port has expanded across the river, and for many miles downstream. The world's biggest lock, at Zandvliet, enables big ships to enter. The need to link both river banks led to the building of the great Kennedy Tunnel. A great deal of the petroleum, upon which Belgian industry depends, is imported through Antwerp.

◄ Antwerp is one of Belgium's greatest and most interesting cities. The house of the painter, Rubens, and the workshop and house of the printer Christopher Plantin, are particularly worth a visit.

▼ The Kennedy Road Tunnel. It links both banks of the Scheldt, which is here over $\frac{1}{4}$ mile wide. It was built, section by section, on dry land. The sections were then lowered onto the bed of the river.

Places to visit in Antwerp

1 Rubens's House

2 Antwerp Cathedral

3 Brabo fountain in the Grote Markt

4 National Maritime Museum, Steen Castle

5 Zoological gardens

6 Sunday-morning bird market

▲ Antwerp Cathedral. This is one of the biggest Gothic churches in the world. Although hemmed in by houses, the tall, delicate spire can be seen for miles.

◄ Antwerp Zoo lies just behind the Central Station. It contains one of the largest collections of rare animals and birds to be found in Europe.

▼ The port of Antwerp stretches for several miles along the river. The Scheldt is wide enough and deep enough to enable all but the biggest ships to reach it, and to make Antwerp one of the world's most important ports.

Language and media

The languages of Belgium

After the Romans withdrew in the fifth century, the desolated lands in the north of Belgium were occupied by tribes of German origin, who spoke a different language from the Belgian tribes in the south.

Today there is still no single Belgian language. In the north, the Flemings speak various Dutch dialects, and Dutch is the official language. In the south, the Walloons speak French.

The language frontier

There was a time when all official business was done in French, and nobody gained a senior job without a perfect knowledge of French, even in the Dutch-speaking areas. The rights of the Dutch speakers have been established only with difficulty. By fixing a language frontier across the country in 1962–3, the Government made it difficult to arrive at any other solution. The existence of two principal languages is an expensive nuisance to a small country.

Belgium has a great many newspapers, of which the biggest are *Le Soir* and *Het Laatste Nieuws*. The Catholic newspaper, *La Libre Belgique*, circulates between the two language groups. Belgium also has two television services, one broadcasting in Dutch and the other in French.

▲ Notices and advertisements are almost invariably in both languages. This is time wasting and expensive, and can be very confusing for foreigners.

▼ Language riots at Louvain in January 1968. The university was bilingual, but Flemish students protested about the privileged position of the Walloons.

▲ A Brussels news kiosk. In addition to a wide selection of papers in French and Dutch, there are enough foreigners to make it worthwhile selling foreign publications.

► A language frontier was established in Belgium in 1962-3. To the north, Dutch is the official language. In the south it is French. Brussels is bilingual. There are two German-speaking regions in the east.

▼ A Belgian cafe with the menu in both Dutch and French.

The Belgian language frontier

German speaking
Bilingual (Dutch and French)
French speaking
Dutch speaking

► A Luxembourg television studio. Programmes can be received in parts of Belgium, where stations are not allowed to broadcast advertisements.

A new role in Europe

The first steps to unity

Belgium emerged from the First World War more respected than ever before, and became one of the first signatories of the League of Nations. Belgium went on to point the way towards international cooperation by forming an economic union (B.L.E.U.) with Luxembourg.

The events of World War II encouraged thoughts of post-war cooperation, and in 1944 Benelux (an economic union of Belgium, the Netherlands and Luxembourg) was born. The early steps were not always easy because Belgian and Dutch interests were not always the same. But Benelux proved the value of cooperation, and in some respects progress was greater in Benelux than in later organizations.

The new Europe

The creation of a truly integrated Europe, which would include Britain, remained the cornerstone of Belgian policy. The steps towards it, such as defence agreements, the creation of the European Iron and Steel Community, and cooperation in the development of atomic energy, were welcomed. But these were all less important than the creation of the European Economic Community (the Common Market) by the Treaty of Rome in 1957. It was appropriate that the headquarters of the E.E.C. should be set up in Brussels.

Belgium took a further step towards becoming the centre of European decision-making in 1967. General de Gaulle ordered the two defence bodies SHAPE (Supreme Headquarters Allied Personnel Europe) and NATO (North Atlantic Treaty Oranization) to leave France. They both moved to Belgium. In the following year, the headquarters of the Iron and Steel Community, and of Euratom, were moved to Brussels.

Luxembourg, too, has had a share in these developments. It shares with Strasbourg the role of being host to the European Parliament. It also houses some sections of the E.E.C.

▲ A meeting of the North Atlantic Treaty Organization. Belgium willingly gave the Organization a new home after General de Gaulle ordered NATO to leave France in the Sixties.

▼ The United Kingdom joins the Common Market. The Prime Minister, Mr Heath, signed the Treaty of Accession in Brussels on January 22nd, 1972. Ireland and Denmark became members at the same time.

The European Community

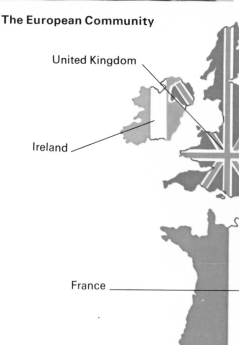

United Kingdom

Ireland

France

► The European Community was created by the six countries who signed the Treaty of Rome in March 1957. In 1972, the United Kingdom, Ireland and Denmark were also admitted. The Community aims at eventual union, and hopes to provide fair shares for all sections of society in the rising prosperity which co-operation would bring.

▼ The Berlaymont Building, Brussels. These offices house hundreds of officials drawn from all the nine member countries. Their job is to make proposals to the Council of Ministers, and to implement decisions.

▲ Judges in session at the European Court of Justice, Luxembourg. The Court is the supreme arbiter in deciding Community law.

▼ Signing the Treaty of Rome, March 25th, 1957. The treaty, signed by the leading ministers of "the Six"—Belgium, France, Germany, Luxembourg, Italy and the Netherlands—brought the Common Market into being.

Denmark

Netherlands

Belgium

West Germany

Luxembourg

Italy

Old crafts and new skills

Steel, guns and glass

When World War II ended, the Belgians were quickly able to restore their industries, because their factories and transport system had suffered little damage. They found ready markets, and Belgium was very prosperous for several years.

However, new problems were arising. Belgium relied upon its old industries—especially coal and steel—and its old factories, while its neighbours were building new, efficient factories and new industries. In spite of this, Belgium remains a very important steel-making country. Two-thirds of its steel is sold abroad, and thousands of firms of all sizes are engaged in making everything from screwdrivers to locomotives.

One craft in which Belgium has established an international reputation is the manufacture of guns. The FN automatic rifle, developed in Belgium, has been adopted by several NATO countries.

Belgium has one of the biggest glass industries in the world. It developed because everything needed was at hand, including products from the important chemical industry. In some branches of glassmaking Belgium has led the world for many years.

Textiles and diamonds

Belgium's textile industry is concentrated mainly around Ghent and Verviers. Belgium's reputation for clothmaking goes back to the Middle Ages. In the manufacture of woollens, Belgium ranks second only to France among the European countries. She was also one of the first countries in the world to manufacture rayon, and now has an important synthetic trade.

The most interesting of Belgium's special trades is diamond cutting. This trade grew up in Antwerp, and the city has become the world centre for trade in cut diamonds. The less valuable diamonds are used by industry to make diamond-headed tools which are used on drills, for example, by the oil industry.

▲ A coal miner at work. The coalfields of the Campine, north of Liège, contain 70% of Belgium's known reserves. Much of the electricity produced in Belgium comes from low-grade coal.

▼ A field of flax. Flax, from which the fine Belgian linen is woven, is widely grown in Flanders. It is the only natural textile which Belgium produces in quantities.

▲ A steel plant in Luxembourg. Luxembourg has rich supplies of iron ore. In Luxembourg and Belgium, steel making is the most important industry.

Some Belgian crafts

▲ Diamond cutting is centred in Antwerp. Antwerp is also the principal world centre for trade in cut diamonds.

▲ Lace making. Some of the lace sold in Belgium is manufactured at home, using old skills which have been handed down.

▼ Part of the oil terminal complex on the Scheldt at Antwerp. The port cannot handle the largest of the oil tankers now in service, but is ideally placed to process the crude oil used by industry.

▲ Cutting patterns on crystal glass. Belgium makes high quality glass as well as flat glass. Its craftsmen are very skilled.

▲ Engraving a shotgun. The manufacture of guns is centred at Liège. Shotguns, used for sport, fetch a very high price.

From motorways to waterways

▼ In many Flemish towns it is often difficult to cross the road at rush hour because of the number of bicycles. Bicycles in Belgium have to be licensed.

Roads and ports

The giant lorries, rolling across Belgium from all parts of Europe, the Middle East and beyond, make it clear that this is the best route, and that Belgium is the crossroads of Western Europe.

Antwerp, Zeebrugge, Ostend and Ghent are four of Europe's most modern ports, handling many types of traffic. The motorway, which crosses underneath the Scheldt by the Kennedy tunnel, is part of the great system which will link northern Europe with the south.

Belgium's waterways and railways

Belgium is fortunate in its rivers and canals, which carry a great deal of traffic. For bulky goods, which do not need to reach their destination quickly, the great river barges are ideal.

The Belgians have shown ingenuity in solving difficult problems. On the Brussels-Charleroi canal at Ronquières is the world's only sloping lock. To overcome a big difference in waterlevel, ships are carried

▼ One of the most recent Belgian trains to be introduced. Its electrified main line service is very good. Its goods trains, which include several diesel locomotives, are very important to industry and trade.

▶ Barges on a Belgian river. In 1971, barges carried a record 95 million tons of freight. Belgium's river system is linked by canals which carry goods over a wide area of the Netherlands, Germany and France.

from one end of the lock to the other in two huge tanks of water which are hauled up or down the slope by powerful diesel engines.

Belgium, which had the first railway on the European continent, now has one of the densest railway networks in the world.

Driving in Belgium

As everywhere, Belgians buy cars because they like them, and they are useful, and they condemn everybody else's car for the nuisance it causes! There was a time when Belgians were considered the world's worst drivers, and the accident rate is still very high. But it is no longer possible to drive without taking a test. It is a serious matter to be caught driving if drunk, and Belgium is one of the first countries to make the wearing of seat belts compulsory.

The bicycle is still an important means of getting about. Hundreds are to be seen parked every day outside factories and at railway stations. Through the towns, and along many roads, especially in Flanders, special paths have been laid for cyclists.

▲ A tram at one of Brussels' new underground stations. The new Metro will take several years to complete. In the meantime, trams run through the finished sections. This saves much congestion on the roads.

▲ One of Belgium's motorways. The motorway system, which has been built to high standards, has made rapid progress in the last decade. It is designed to form part of the great European system.

▼ SABENA and LUXAIR are the national air lines of Belgium and Luxembourg respectively. SABENA is the bigger of the two, and has some 70 overseas routes serving 50 countries in four continents. The size of Luxembourg airport puts serious limitations on the size of aircraft which LUXAIR can use.

Invention and discovery

Bathyscaphe

▶ Professor Auguste Piccard (1884-1962) of Brussels University, was a pioneer explorer of the upper atmosphere and of the ocean depths. In 1931, he reached a height, by balloon, of 15,500 metres (50,853 ft.) and in the next year a record ocean depth. His son Jacques (1914-) reached a new record depth of 11 km. (7 miles) in the Pacific Ocean in 1960. To withstand the great pressures, he and his companion descended in a specially constructed bathyscaphe.

The development of industry

By the middle of the nineteenth century, Belgium had become an industrial nation, and was taking an important part in the development of new processes. Although the names of some of the inventors are not well-known, their work was important, and sometimes led to the development of new Belgian industries.

One such person was Ernest Solvay, who developed a soda manufacturing process in 1863, which still bears his name. At about the same time, Daniel Dony, a Liège chemist, developed a new method of separating zinc. Today, Belgium is among the world's leading exporters of non-ferrous metals. Better known is the work of L. H. Baekeland, who invented bakelite, a form of moulded plastic.

Belgian researchers

In modern science, many researchers are usually working in the same field. Zénobe Gramme (1826–1901), who built the first industrial dynamo, was engaged in research which made the name of the German, Siemens, even more famous.

Etienne Lenoir, whose monument can be seen in Arlon, made important discoveries in the development of the petrol engine, but another thirty years went by before the Germans Daimler and Benz put the petrol engine into a motor car.

Mercator's projection

▲ Gerard Mercator, born in Rupelmonde in 1512, is famous as a mapmaker. Mercator's projection "flattened" the globe by making cuts from the Poles towards the Equator. Some countries look much too big, but the important parts of the world of his day were least distorted.

Adolphe Sax

▲ Adolphe Sax (1814-94), the inventor of the saxophone, was born in Dinant. His earliest saxophone was very different from those used by orchestras now, but the principle was the same.

Early cornet designed by Sax

Modern saxophone

Vesalius

▼ Vesalius (Andreas van Wessels, 1514-64) turned the study of anatomy into a science. He rejected the notion that the ancient Greeks knew everything about the human body. His great work, *De Humani Corporis Fabrica,* was based on his own observations.

► An illustration from *De Humani Corporis Fabrica*

Christopher Plantin

▼ The Plantin Museum, Antwerp. Christopher Plantin (c. 1520-89) founded one of the greatest printing houses of his period. His masterpiece was a polyglot Bible. The modern typeface named after him (right) is based on one of his.

abcdefghijklmnop
qrstuvwxyz
ABCDEFGHIJKLMNO
PQRSTUVWXYZ
1234567890 .,;:?!-'&£

Heroes in fact and fiction

▼ The Toone Puppets. The puppet theatre is hidden away in a narrow alley in the oldest part of Brussels. The play, which is changed every month, is performed in a local dialect.

Early leaders

The Belgians have always had great admiration for leaders who have roused the people to defend themselves against the enemy. In Tongeren, a fine statue of Ambiorix stands in the main square. It was he who led the tribes of the Belgae in revolt against the Romans.

Godfrey of Bouillon, whose castle can still be seen in the Ardennes, earned fame as a leader of the First Crusade. He was elected King of Jerusalem in 1099, but refused to wear a golden crown in a city where Christ wore a crown of thorns.

Heroes of the people

Although he was much less famous, many Belgians know about Everard t'Serclaes (1320–88). He was a deputy mayor of Brussels, who was murdered while defend-

▲ Cardinal Mercier, Archbishop of Malines, (1851-1925) took a leading part during the First World War in building Belgian morale to resist the enemy. The Germans did not dare to imprison him, as a leading churchman.

◄ Interior of the Erasmus House, Brussels. The great scholar paid frequent visits to Brussels, and from about 1525 stayed in the house, which belonged to his friend Canon Wichmann. The house is now a museum of Erasmus's life and works.

ing the city. During the Second World War, when German troops occupied Brussels, people made a practice of visiting his monument, and touched the brass figure as a mark of respect. Today, hundreds of visitors come to the site, and continue to touch the figure for luck.

The First World War produced national heroes. Adolphe Max, the Mayor of Brussels, openly encouraged people to defy the Germans for a whole month before he was arrested and sent to prison. His place was taken by Cardinal Mercier, Archbishop of Malines, who ordered the priests to read out a letter calling upon people to support their King and ignore the enemy. He kept the German governor standing whenever he called, and it was only in November 1918, when Germany had been defeated, that he offered the Governor a chair.

▲ Tintin and his dog. This famous cartoon character was created by the Belgian artist, Hergé. Since he first appeared, his adventures have been followed in newspapers, books, and on television by children everywhere.

▶ Georges Simenon, who was born in Liège, wrote a series of detective novels featuring the famous character Inspector Maigret. Many of the novels have been dramatized. On the right is a scene from a television series in which the actor Rupert Davies played the part of Inspector Maigret.

▲ Adolphe Max drinks a glass of beer with King Albert after the Germans had been driven out of Belgium. As deputy mayor of Brussels, he had been imprisoned in 1914 for calling on the population to resist the Germans.

▶ The monument to Everard t'Serclaes, near a corner of the Grand' Place, Brussels, is visited by many people. The brass figure, and the nose of his dog, have become shiny where people have touched them to bring good luck.

The Belgian character

A middle class society

There are very rich Belgians, and there are very poor ones, too. But Belgian society is above all middle class. There is a Minister for the Middle Classes in the Government.

As a nation, Belgians are very hard-working. They believe in giving, and getting, good value. They often seem to be interested only in material things. For many people everyday life may be dull, but when they get the opportunity to enjoy themselves, they enter into the spirit of it with great enthusiasm.

Conservatism and stability

According to the newspapers, Belgium appears to be beset with many problems and disputes, but it is really a very conservative country. New, small political parties attract attention from time to time, but it is really the three main parties who dominate the scene.

The great influence of the Catholic Church makes for stability. It affects people's ordinary lives, too. It is difficult for a person, having chosen to belong to a party, to change his politics. Many of the things he does, such as the union he joins and the club he belongs to, have their links with the Church and politics.

A nation of individualists

Most Belgians are individualists, preferring their own company and that of their close friends. This makes it difficult for foreigners to get to know Belgians socially. This attitude spills over into public life. Small communities prefer to run their own affairs, and most people are suspicious of authority. Life in Belgium, however, is changing, and the attitudes of young people are often very different from those of their parents.

A contrast is often made between the shorter, dark, volatile Walloon of the south and the taller, fair-haired, dour Fleming. But this, in spite of their political differences, can be exaggerated. Intermarriage obscures many differences. Above all, they are Belgians, and when the honour and dignity of their country is at stake, they react as one.

▼ To Belgians any current of air is a draught. In summer they would often prefer to swelter rather than open a window. Foreigners in Belgium look forward to the day when air conditioning is universal!

◄ Like the Germans, Belgians shake hands on every conceivable occasion. It would not be unusual for an office worker to shake hands all round with his colleagues in the room, and perhaps on some other occasion during the day as well.

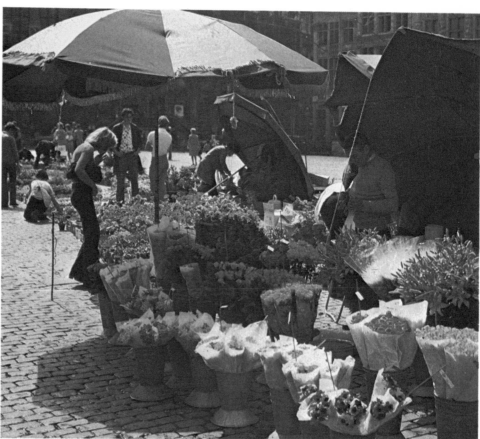

▲ A Brussels flower market. The daily flower market in the Grand' Place is open from 9 a.m. to 4 p.m. With the gaily-coloured umbrellas under which the traders sit, the market makes a brilliant foreground to the ancient buildings.

▲ A Sunday afternoon cycle race in a provincial town. Young men train hard for the honour of winning local races even when the prizes are small.

◄ The rush to get home. Belgians are not used to forming a queue, and tram entrances often get blocked. Oddly, people do not usually protest loudly when somebody cheats to get on.

▼ Good food matters a great deal to Belgians. During the low season, proprietors fill their hotels by arranging "gastronomic weekends". Celebrated chefs are invited to prepare special dishes. It costs much less to buy a bag of chipped potatoes or a waffle from a stall in the street.

The Belgian influence

The Flemish influence

Between about the thirteenth and sixteenth centuries, Flanders was the major centre of the artistic and commercial life of Western Europe.

The splendid cloth, which the Flemings wove from fine English wool, found buyers everywhere. Flemish towns grew to replace the great annual fairs, which had once met Europe's needs. The Flemish towns grew rich on two-way commerce, which reached to the most distant parts. Flemish seamen were feared, if not respected, over the whole of the North Sea.

The descendants of those who made money spent freely, and the wonderful architecture of the old towns and the art of the Flemish school are permanent heritages. In later years, when conditions in Flanders became difficult, many people from these parts carried their skills with them when seeking new homes in England and elsewhere.

In modern times, Belgium has played a part out of proportion to her size. Queen Victoria was particularly annoyed that the Belgians should have minds of their own. At one point, she wrote to the Belgian King, "I cannot at all see HOW you can *even* entertain the question, for, as I just said, the *basis* of the *existence* of Belgium is her neutrality".

The Congo

King Leopold II realized the importance and wealth of Africa at a time when European nations were content to establish trading posts. In 1885, with the advice of the explorer Stanley, Leopold established a vast colony in the Congo as his own private venture. The new colony was rich in rubber and ivory. In 1908, the Belgian government assumed responsibility for the Congo, following protests against the treatment of the native Congolese. The colony achieved independence in 1960.

It has been in Europe that her statesmen, such as Paul-Henri Spaak and Jean Rey, have helped Belgium to make her greatest contribution by promoting the unity of Western Europe.

▲ Assembling stained glass. Belgium has one of the biggest glass industries in the world. The industry includes the manufacture of blown-glass, crystal, and the design of stained glass.

▲ Jacques Feyder (1888-1948) the Belgian film producer. In 1935, he produced the classic *Kermesse Heroïque*. As Belgium has no major film industry of its own, he worked in Paris.

▼ *Shepherds adoring the Lamb,* by Van der Goes (c. 1445-82). His best work is in Florence. He would be better known as a Flemish painter if more of his paintings were in Belgium.

▲ Belgian merchants in the Middle Ages made the Low Countries among the richest areas in Europe. The fine woollen cloth they sold was prized everywhere.

◄ King Baudouin I and Queen Fabiola. Baudouin succeeded his father after the latter had been forced to abdicate. The Crown has since regained much of its respect.

▼ Patrice Lumumba and Joseph Kasavubu, respectively Prime Minister and Head of State of the Congo, following the granting of independence in 1960.

▲ Paul-Henri Spaak (1899-1972), the first president of the U.N. General Assembly. He was twice Belgian Prime Minister, and six times Foreign Minister. He was an architect of European integration.

Progress and prosperity

Non aux villes inhumaines !...

▶ One of many posters to be seen, urging Belgians to preserve and modernize old buildings instead of tearing them down to make room for tall office blocks.

.▼ The Nuclear Energy Study Centre, at Mol, near Antwerp. It has three large reactors, and is designed to train specialists in nuclear research. It was founded in 1947 and employs some 1,200 staff.

The problems of prosperity

In Brussels great office blocks are being built, and for a long time traffic has had to cope with major roadworks in the city centre. These changes have done nothing to make Brussels more beautiful, and essential changes have not always been carefully planned. In many parts of Flanders, new factories with well-known foreign names are to be seen. This all points to Belgium's growing prosperity, and to its new role in Europe.

Changes in Flanders

One big change has been more subtle. Many of the new industries have grown up in the Flemish area of the north, while the older industries in the south have not shown the same progress. As their region has become richer and more important, the Flemish people have become more outspoken.

▲ Commuters arriving at the Central Railway Station, Brussels, to begin another day's work. Many people travel to the capital each day, attracted by the higher wages. The development of Belgium's excellent railways enables them to commute longer distances.

The days when the Flemings were mainly farm labourers, and the French-speaking Walloons were better educated and able to command the best jobs, have now gone. The Flemings have won many important rights.

New industries

The development of new industries has been rapid, and none has grown faster since the War than the oil industry. Belgium's oil refineries support an important petro-chemical industry. Belgium has not been slow to move towards nuclear energy. Two large nuclear power stations are being developed at Doel and Tihange.

Belgium has always been a meeting place for foreign people and foreign cultures. This is so today because of Belgium's growing importance in international business and politics.

▲ An American-owned petroleum refinery at Feluy, near Mons. This side of Belgian industry has made very rapid progress since the days when Belgium was merely a distributor of imported gasoline.

▼ The Sidmar steelworks at Zelzate in East Flanders. Scrap metal is being added to the converter. Antwerp is conveniently near as a source of iron ore and for the shipment of finished products.

► Mealtime at a day nursery in Brussels. Many children up to the age of three can be left at a day nursery if the mother goes out to work or is ill. Belgium has established a fine record in providing such schools as part of its social services.

Reference
Human and physical geography

The climate of Belgium and Luxembourg

Annual rainfall of Belgium

- 70–90 cm.
- 90–110 cm.
- 110–140 cm.
- Over 140 cm.

FACTS AND FIGURES: BELGIUM

Full title: Royaume de Belgique (French). Koninkrijk België (Dutch).
Position: Between 2 and 6 E and 49, 50 and 51 50 N. Borders on France, the Duchy of Luxembourg, West Germany and the Netherlands.
Capital: Brussels.
Area: 30,506 sq. km. (11,778 sq. miles).
Population: 9,727,000 (1972). 5,478,000 are Flemish (Dutch speaking). 3,117,000 are Walloon (French speaking). Greater Brussels, which is officially bilingual, has a population of 1,071,000.
Languages: French, Dutch and German are all official languages.
Religion: Most Belgians are Roman Catholics. There are about 24,000 Protestants and 35,000 Jews.
Political system: A parliamentary democracy in which all Belgian men and women, over the age of 21, have the right to vote.
Armed forces: Total: approx. 94,000. Compulsory service lasts for 12 months for privates and 15 months for voluntary reserve officers.

The climate of Belgium is, on the whole, temperate and similar to that of Britain. The average rainfall is about 83 cm. (32 inches), but it is much higher in the hilly Ardennes region of the south east. Early winter is usually the wettest time of the year. Belgians are very conscious of the drizzle, which seems so often to fall, and *"La drache nationale"* has become a national joke. Fog and mist are common in the damp, low-lying areas of Flanders away from the coast, as a result of the cooling of the night air.

Brussels

The natural vegetation of Belgium and Luxembourg

Desert Vegetation
Sandy Coastal Wastes

Grass Vegetation
Peat & Sandy Polderland

Shrub, Heath & Marshy Grassland

Meadowland

Fertile Grassland

Valley Grassland

Forest Vegetation
Mixed Broad-leaved & Coniferous Woodland & Meadow

FACTS AND FIGURES: LUXEMBOURG

Full title: Grand Duché de Luxembourg.
Position: Approx. 6 E and between 49 50 and 50 20 N. The Grand Duchy of Luxembourg must not be confused with the Belgian province of Luxembourg.
Capital: Luxembourg City.
Area: 2,586 sq. km. (999 sq. miles).
Population: 352,000 (1973). The capital has a population of 78,300.
Language: Luxemburgish (a German dialect not spoken elsewhere). French, German and English are widely used.
Religion: Roman Catholic. In 1960, there were 2,951 Protestants and 643 Jews.
Political system: A constitutional monarchy. Citizens, over the age of 18, have a right to elect the members of the Chamber of Deputies.
Armed forces: A battalion-sized army of volunteers.

The population density

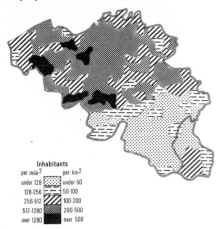

Inhabitants

per mile²	per km²
under 128	under 50
128-256	50-100
256-512	100-200
512-1280	200-500
over 1280	over 500

Belgium is one of the most densely populated areas of Europe. It has a population density of roughly 315 people per square kilometre (810 per square mile). Of the population of about 9.7 million, about 600,000 are foreigners. Growing prosperity has resulted in large towns gaining at the expense of smaller townships. Five towns—Brussels, Antwerp, Liège, Ghent and Charleroi—have well over a quarter of the total population. The Flemish provinces have about 55% of the population and the Walloons 33%. The density of population is twice as great among the Flemings.

The Belgian system of government

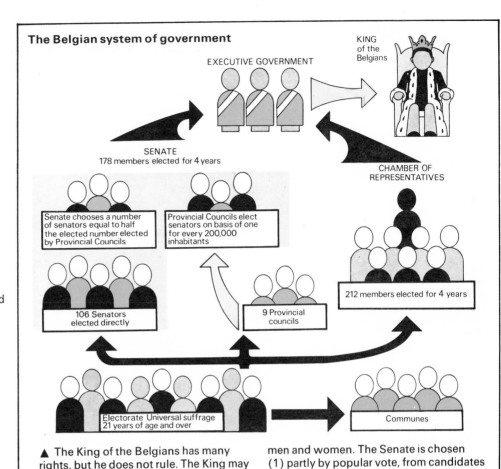

EXECUTIVE GOVERNMENT

KING of the Belgians

SENATE
178 members elected for 4 years

CHAMBER OF REPRESENTATIVES

Senate chooses a number of senators equal to half the elected number elected by Provincial Councils

Provincial Councils elect senators on basis of one for every 200,000 inhabitants

212 members elected for 4 years

106 Senators elected directly

9 Provincial councils

Electorate Universal suffrage 21 years of age and over

Communes

▲ The King of the Belgians has many rights, but he does not rule. The King may dissolve Parliament, and appoint and dismiss ministers. If a government falls, it is his job to find a minister to form a new government. Parliament consists of two Houses, both with similar powers. The House of Representatives is elected by all men and women. The Senate is chosen (1) partly by popular vote, from candidates who belong to bodies such as professional organizations or trade unions; (2) partly from nominations by the Provincial Councils; and (3) partly from nominations by the senators themselves.

Population of principal towns

1972 estimates

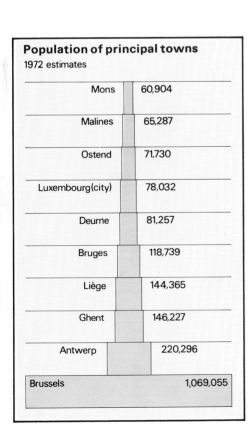

Mons	60,904
Malines	65,287
Ostend	71,730
Luxembourg (city)	78,032
Deurne	81,257
Bruges	118,739
Liège	144,365
Ghent	146,227
Antwerp	220,296
Brussels	1,069,055

The Luxembourg system of government

Council of State
21 members chosen for life by Sovereign

Grand Duke

Chamber of Deputies

President of Government, Minister of State, and at least 3 ministers

56 members elected for 5 years

Executive

Electorate   4 electoral districts

▲ The present Grand Duke, Jean, has been sovereign since 1964 when his mother abdicated. The Crown is hereditary in the House of Nassau. The Grand Duke appoints the Prime Minister, whose government must consist of at least three other ministers. Legislative power is in the hands of a Council of State, appointed by the sovereign, and a Chamber of Deputies elected by the people of Luxembourg. Both the Chamber of Deputies and the Duke and his Ministers may submit matters to the Council of State for discussion.

Reference
History

MAIN EVENTS IN HISTORY

B.C.

c. 500 — Belgic tribes move into area now known as Belgium.

50 — Roman occupation of region after revolt by Ambiorix is crushed.

A.D.

407 — Withdrawal of Roman forces. Northern part of country occupied by people of Germanic origin.

c. 500 — Merovingian king begins long process of uniting all of Gaul, including Belgian lands.

800 — Belgium becomes part of Charlemagne's Holy Roman Empire. Empire breaks up on Charlemagne's death in 814.

843 — Treaty of Verdun makes Belgium part of Lotharingia.

879 — Lotharingia absorbed by Germany.

9th-12th centuries — Absence of firm rule leads to rise of powerful local rulers.

12th-14th centuries — Flemish towns grow rich and powerful.

1302 — Battle of Golden Spurs. Flemish craftsmen defeat the French to preserve independence.

1346 — Louis de Mâle becomes Count of Flanders.

1357 — Louis invades Brabant and becomes Duke of Brabant.

THE BURGUNDIAN PERIOD

1369 — Louis's heiress, Margaret, marries Philip the Bold, Duke of Burgundy.

1384 — Margaret inherits Flanders, Antwerp, Malines and territories in France.

1390 — Brabant ceded to Duke Philip.

1393 — Limburg ceded to Duke Philip.

1404 — John the Fearless succeeds as Duke of Burgundy.

1419 — Accession of Philip the Good of Burgundy.

1438-56 — Bruges, Ghent and Liège forced to surrender many of their liberties.

1443 — Philip buys Luxembourg.

1467-77 — Reign of Charles the Bold of Burgundy.

1477 — Marriage of Charles's daughter, Mary, to Archduke Maximilian.

THE HAPSBURG PERIOD

1482 — Death of Mary. Maximilian becomes Regent over possessions in Low Countries.

1486-92 — Low Countries subdued, except for bishopric of Liège.

1494 — Maximilian's son, Philip the Fair, assumes control in Low Countries.

1500 — Charles V, son of Philip, born in Ghent.

1506 — Charles succeeds Philip.

1516 — Charles V becomes King of Spain.

1529 — Charles V inherits Austria.

1537-8 — Revolt of Ghent.

1555 — Charles V abdicates. Accession of Philip II of Spain.

1555-58 — Growing opposition to Spanish troops in Low Countries and to position of Catholic Church.

1559 — Margaret of Parma appointed governor.

THE REVOLT OF THE NETHERLANDS

1569 — Revolt of the Sea Beggars on Flemish coast.

1572 — Sea Beggars capture Brill. Flemish towns badly hit by restriction on seaborne trade.

1576 — Antwerp sacked by Spanish mutineers.

1577-87 — Spaniards re-establish authority.

1598 — Death of Philip II. Flanders acquires semi-independence.

1648 — Peace of Münster. Dutch retain Flemish Zealand and North Brabant and declare the Scheldt closed.

BELGIUM AS A BATTLEGROUND

1667-8 — War of Devolution. French capture Tournai.

1679-84 — Louis XIV annexes Walloon Flanders and half of Hainaut.

1692 — Namur captured by French. Retaken in 1695.

1702-13 — War of Spanish Succession. Belated efforts by Spanish to improve conditions in Low Countries hampered by campaigns of Marlborough and Prince Eugene.

1713 — French abandon claim on the Southern Netherlands to Austria.

1740-48 — War of Austrian Succession.

1747 — Belgium occupied by the French. Restored to Austria by Treaty of Aix-la-Chapelle.

1790 — All the provinces, except Luxembourg, declare independence from Austria, under title of "United States of Belgium". Collapses after two years.

1794 — Following defeat of Austrians, Belgium is incorporated into French Republic.

1804-14 — Reign of Napoleon I. Scheldt re-opened to shipping, and French legal code introduced.

1814 — Treaty of London. Belgium and Luxembourg united with Netherlands under Dutch King.

1815 — Battle of Waterloo. William I crowned King of United Netherlands in Brussels.

1830 — Belgian revolt against pro-Dutch policies of William I. Independence of Belgium is recognised by Great Powers.

THE KINGDOM OF BELGIUM

1831 — Leopold of Saxe-Coburg is crowned King of the Belgians. Dutch refuse to recognise new Kingdom. French forces called in to expel Dutch from Antwerp.

1838 — Dutch agree to recognise independence of Belgium.

1839 — Treaty of London. Independence and neutrality of Belgium is guaranteed. Belgium surrenders parts of N. Flanders and Limburg to Netherlands.

1861-3 — Belgium makes free trade agreements with several nations.

1863 — Belgium buys right of free navigation on Scheldt from Netherlands.

1865 — Death of Leopold I. Accession of Leopold II.

1878 — Leopold's interest in colonies leads to formation of committee to study problems of the Congo.

1881 — Leopoldville established in the Congo.

1885 — Congo becomes a new State, as a private venture by the King.

1908 — Congo becomes a Belgian colony.

1909 — Death of Leopold II. Accession of his nephew, Albert I.

WORLD WAR I

1914 — Aug. 4: Germany invades Belgium.
Aug. 20: German troops enter Brussels.
Aug. 23: Battle of Mons.
Oct. 9: Antwerp surrenders.
Oct. 30-Nov. 24: First Battle of Ypres.

1918 — Nov. 22: Albert I and Belgian troops re-enter Brussels after withdrawal of Germans.

BETWEEN THE WARS

1926 — Locarno Treaty guarantees Belgian frontiers.

1934 — Feb. 17: Death of Albert I. Accession of Leopold III.

1936 — April: Belgium substitutes policy of independent action for position of neutrality.

1937 — Britain and France promise Belgium assistance if invaded.

WORLD WAR II

1940 — Jan.: Belgium refuses permission for Britain and France to station forces there, after discovery of German plans to invade Belgium.
May 10: German forces attack Belgium without warning. Belgium is quickly over-run.

May 28: King makes unconditional surrender. Belgian Government forms Government-in-exile.

1944 British, Canadian and allied troops are given task of recapturing Antwerp and advancing into Belgium. Sept. 3: Brussels liberated. Government-in-exile returns, Sept. 8th.

1945 May: Unconditional surrender of Germany.

EVENTS SINCE 1945
1945-50 Controversy over future of exiled King Leopold. A referendum favours his return.

1951 Opposition forces King to abdicate. Succeeded by son, Baudouin I.

1960 June: Congo granted independence.

1968 French-speaking faculties of the University of Louvain moved to Ottignies after language riots.

1970 May: King Baudouin visits Zaïre (Congo) and signs a treaty of friendship and cooperation.

EUROPEAN UNITY
1921 Economic Union between Belgium and Luxembourg agreed.

1948 Union enlarged to include Netherlands (Benelux).

1949 Belgium signs Treaty of London leading to establishment of Council of Europe. Belgium becomes member of North Atlantic Treaty Organization (NATO).

1951 Establishment of European Coal and Steel Community between Belgium, France, Italy, West Germany, the Netherlands and Luxembourg.

1957 Treaty of Rome brings European Economic Community (Common Market) into being. Belgium joins European Atomic Energy Community (Euratom).

1967 Belgium offers home to NATO and SHAPE.

1968 Headquarters of Common Market, Euratom, and Iron and Steel Community grouped in Brussels.

The Arts

LITERATURE
Conscience, Hendrick (1812-83). Revived literary Flemish: *The Lion of Flanders*.
Pirmez, Octave (1823-83). Mystical meditations: *Les Heures de Philosophie*.
De Coster, Charles (1827-79). Novelist: *La Légende de Uylenspiegel*.
Gezelle, Guido (1830-99). Lyric poet who wrote in Dutch.
Verhaeren, Emile (1855-1916). Poet: *La Ville Tentaculaire*.
Pirenne, Henri (1862-1949). Historian of international fame.
Maeterlinck, Maurice (1862-1916). Nobel prizewinner: *The Blue-bird, Pelléas et Mélisande*.
Lateur, Frank (Stijn Steuvels) (1871-). *De Vlaschaard*.
Woestijne, Karl van de (1878-1929). Poet and essayist.
Feirlinck, H. (1879-1967). Novelist: *Het Gevecht met de Engel*.
Plisnier, Charles (1896-1952). Short stories and novels in French: *Faux Passeports*.
Ghilderode, Michel de (1899-1962). Dramatist: *Fastes d'Enfer*.
Goris, Jan-Albert (Marnix Gijsen) (1889-). Novels, poems and essays in Dutch.
Simenon, Georges (1903-). Novelist. Creator of the Maigret detective novels.
Boon, Louis Paul (1912-). Novelist who sympathizes with the outsider in society.
Mallet-Joris, Françoise (1930-). Novelist. Won Femina Prize, 1958.

PAINTING
Van Eyck, Jan (1365-1440). Flemish artist who developed the use of oil painting. Major works include the Ghent altarpiece and *Portrait of Giovanni Arnolfini and wife*.
Van Eyck, Hubert (c. 1366-1426). Central panel of Ghent altarpiece, *Adoration of the Lamb*.
Flémalle, Master of (perhaps Campin, Robert c. 1378-1444). Mérode altarpiece.
Van der Weyden, Rogier (1399-1464). Altarpieces: *Descent from the Cross, The Seven Sacraments, Last Judgement*.
Bouts, Dirk (c. 1415-75). Altarpiece: *The Holy Sacrament*.
Memling, Hans (1433-94). Paintings on reliquary of St. Ursula.
Bosch, Hieronymus (c. 1450-1516). *The Last Judgement, The Temptation of St. Anthony*. Many paintings for secret Flemish brotherhood.
Massys, Quentin (1466-1530). Introduced Italian influence into Flemish art. *Lamentation over Dead Christ*.
Orley, Bernard van (1488-1541). Cartoons for tapestry: *The Entombment*.

Brueghel, Pieter the Elder (c. 1525-69). Many paintings of contemporary Flemish life, often in protest at Spanish excesses.
Rubens, Paul (1577-1648). Portrait painter and landscape artist. *Adoration of the Magi, Fall of the Damned*.
Jordaens, Jacob (1593-1678). Pictures of merrymaking among gods and common folk.
Van Dyck, Anthony (1599-1641). Portraitist. Court painter to Charles I of England.
Teniers, David, the younger (1610-90). Genre painter.
Redouté, Pierre Joseph (1759-1840). Luxembourg artist, famous for flower-paintings.
Wouters, Rik (1822-1916). Dynamic colours and dematerialized forms.
Pernicke, Constant (1886-1952). Expressionist painter who specialized in Flemish peasants and landscapes.
Ensor, James (1860-1949). Expressionist painter: *Entry of Christ into Brussels*.
Masereel, Franz (1889-). Specialized in woodcuts.
Magritte, René (1898-). Surrealist artist.

ARCHITECTURE AND DECORATIVE ARTS
Vriendt, Cornelis de (1514-75). Antwerp town hall, choir screen of Tournai cathedral.
Meunier, Constantin (1831-1905). Sculptor who rebelled against classical tradition: *The Hammerman*.
Velde, Henry van der (1863-1957). Leader of "art nouveau" movement.
Horta, Baron Victor (1861-1947). Prominent in "art nouveau" movement.
Minne, George (1866-1941). Leading figure in "art nouveau" movement.

MUSIC
Binchois, Gilles (c. 1400-60). Rondeaux and hymns.
Dufay, Guillaume (c. 1400-74). Motets and hymns.
Prés, Josquin des (c. 1450-1521). Motets, masses and songs.
Willaert, Adrian (1490-1562). Madrigals, motets and songs.
Lassus, Roland de (c. 1562-94). Psalms and secular music.
Grétry, André (1741-1813). Light operas: *Zémire et Azor*.
Franck, César (1822-90). Symphonies and piano works.
Lekue, Guillaume (1870-94). Outstanding pupil of César Franck.

CINEMA PRODUCERS
Feyder, Jacques (1888-1948). Work includes *La Kermesse Heroïque*.
Rouleau, Raymond (1904-). Produced *The Witches of Salem*.

Agriculture in Belgium and Luxembourg

Imports and exports 1972

Source: O.E.C.D. Economic Surveys B.L.E.U. (1974)

EXPORTS (Million U.S. dollars): Food and live animals 1,393; Beverages and tobacco 88; Crude materials, inedible, exc. fuels 563; Mineral fuels, lubricants etc. 466; Animal and vegetable oils and fats 50; Chemicals 1,564; Manufactured goods classified chiefly by material 6,554; Machinery and transport equipment 3,708; Misc. manufactured articles 1,402

IMPORTS (Million U.S. dollars): Food and live animals 1,682; Beverages and tobacco 225; Crude materials, inedible, exc. fuels 1,447; Mineral fuels, lubricants etc. 1,567; Animal and vegetable oils and fats 100; Chemicals 1,213; Manufactured goods classified chiefly by material 3,636; Machinery and transport equipment 4,359; Misc. manufactured articles 1,345

▲ Belgium is an important trading country. She exports about 40 per cent of her total industrial output. At the same time, she has to import many of the raw materials used. Belgium, therefore, has to depend very much upon world markets, and imports and exports are vital to her existence. Luxembourg's trade is less complicated, but her exports are vital to ensure a high standard of living.

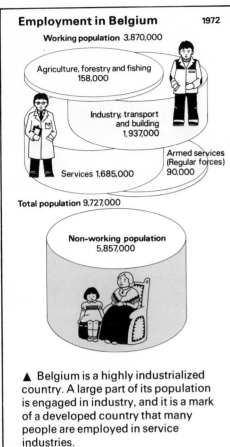

Employment in Belgium 1972

Working population 3,870,000

Agriculture, forestry and fishing 158,000

Industry, transport and building 1,937,000

Services 1,685,000

Armed services (Regular forces) 90,000

Total population 9,727,000

Non-working population 5,857,000

▲ Belgium is a highly industrialized country. A large part of its population is engaged in industry, and it is a mark of a developed country that many people are employed in service industries.

Industry in Belgium and Luxembourg

Symbol	Legend
	Major Industrial Centres
	Mechanical Engineering
	Electrical Engineering
	Shipbuilding
	Railway Equipment
	Motor Vehicles
	Motorcycles
	Rubber Products
	Paper
	Furniture
	Leather Goods
	Shoes
	Glass
	Pottery
	Sugar Refineries
	Tobacco Manufacturing
	Principal Coalmining Areas
	Iron & Steel
	Chemicals
	Oil Refineries
	Textile Districts
	Breweries
	Wine
	Diamond Polishing

The rise in prices and incomes

*Industrial male workers

Industrial Wages *

Retail Prices

Source: Bulletin de Statistique, 1975

▲ Belgium has felt the effects of inflation, and both wages and prices have soared. The wages of industrial workers have risen more than most. The Government attempted to limit wage rises by controlling price rises in 1975.

Goods and services compared to other countries

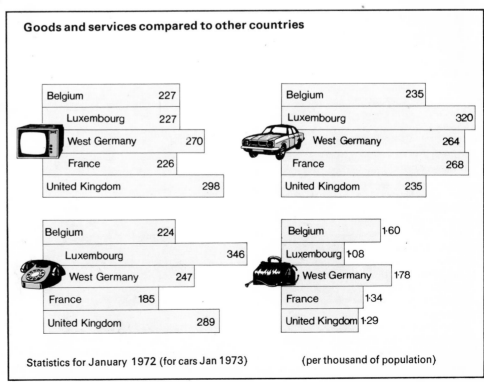

Belgium	227
Luxembourg	227
West Germany	270
France	226
United Kingdom	298

Belgium	235
Luxembourg	320
West Germany	264
France	268
United Kingdom	235

Belgium	224
Luxembourg	346
West Germany	247
France	185
United Kingdom	289

Belgium	1·60
Luxembourg	1·08
West Germany	1·78
France	1·34
United Kingdom	1·29

Statistics for January 1972 (for cars Jan 1973)   (per thousand of population)

Gazetteer

Aalst (50 58N 4 2E). Weaving and brewing centre on R. Dendre. Important for cultivation of hops, and market-gardening. Pop. 46,000.

Antwerp (51 14N 4 23E). Chief Belgian seaport, and major communications centre. Important industries include oil and sugar refining, flour milling and car assembly. Centre of diamond trade. Pop. 217,000.

Ardennes (50 10N 5 40E). High plateau in S.E. Belgium, extending into Luxembourg and France. Fine woodlands, but mainly heath and poor pasture. Centre for sport and hunting. World War II battlegrounds.

Arlon (49 40N 5 47E). One of the oldest towns in Belgium. Roman remains include town wall.

Bastogne (50 0N 5 42E). Rural centre near Luxembourg frontier. Famous for American action in World War II.

Bouillon (49 47N 5 48E). Small Ardennes holiday resort on R. Semoy. Castle of Godfrey of Bouillon overlooks the town.

Bruges (51 13N 3 12E). Most famous of Belgium's medieval towns. Old buildings, canals and bridges make it an important tourist centre. Handmade lace is an important minor industry. Pop. 119,000.

Brussels (50 51N 4 21E). Capital of Belgium. Important commercial and industrial centre. Headquarters of European Economic Community (the Common Market). Many notable buildings in old quarter around Grand' Place. Pop. 1,063,000.

Charleroi (50 28N 4 28E). Major industrial town. Coal mining, steel, iron and glass manufacturing. Heavy electrical engineering. Brewing. Town named after Charles II of Spain.

Courtrai (50 50N 3 15E). Centre of textile industry. Manufactures linen, cotton, nylon, rayon and lace. French defeated in Battle of the Spurs, 1302. Pop. 44,000.

Dinant (50 18N 4 58E). Picturesque tourist centre on R. Meuse. At one time famous for manufacture of copper and brassware.

Esch-sur-Alzette (49 27N 6 00E). Centre of Luxembourg steel industry. Large fertilizer plant. Second largest town in the Duchy. Pop. 27,000.

Ettelbruck (49 51N 6 5E). Major Luxembourg road and rail centre.

Eupen (50 38N 6 3E). German-speaking town, ceded to Belgium in 1918. Manufactures woollen goods and cables.

Genk (50 58N 5 30E). Developed rapidly after World War I, following opening of neighbouring coalfields. Population includes many foreigners who work in mines. Manufactures heavy mining machinery. Pop. 59,000.

Ghent (51 4N 3 43E). One of the most important of Belgium's medieval cities. Many art treasures. Opening of ship canal has made it a major port. Industries include textiles, chemicals, glassware, paper and sugar refining. Pop. 144,000.

Hasselt (50 56N 5 20E). Developed industrially as result of opening of Campine coalfields. Important grain and cattle markets. Brewing and distilling. Tobacco and chicory are cultivated in district. Pop. 40,000.

Huy (50 51N 5 15E). On R. Meuse. Obtained one of the first civic charters in Europe. Famous as home of Peter the Hermit, who proposed the first Crusade.

Liège (50 39N 5 34E). University town and important cultural centre of French-speaking Belgium. Major industrial town. Centre of Belgian metal and armament industries, depending upon coal and iron of neighbourhood, and good transport facilities. Pop. 143,000.

Lier (51 8N 4 32E). Ancient commercial town. Agricultural centre, with small textile industry. Centre of the Flemish political movement. *Liersche Vlaaien* (cooked pastries) speciality of town. Pop. 28,000.

Louvain (50 53N 4 41E). Ancient university town. Famous medieval town-hall. Centre of agricultural district. Industries include brewing and engineering. Pop. 31,000.

Luxembourg City (49 36N 6 7E). Capital of Grand Duchy of Luxembourg. Built on plateau surrounding ravine through which flows R. Alzette. Home of some international bodies, including the European Court of Justice, European Monetary Fund, European Parliament (shared with Strasbourg). Pop. 78,000.

Malines (51 2N 4 27E). Tourist centre with many interesting buildings. Cathedral famous for carillon of bells and its Van Dyck painting of Crucifixion. Once famous for lace-making. Important market-gardening centre. Industries include engineering and car-assembly. Pop. 65,000.

Malmédy (50 26N 6 3E). Small industrial town with tanneries, paper mills and breweries. Ceded by Germany to Belgium after World War I. Almost totally destroyed in fighting in 1944, and now rebuilt.

Mons (50 28E 3 57E). Centre of important coalmining region. Industries include chemicals, brewing, engineering and textiles. Scene of first fighting between British and German armies in World War I. Pop. 62,000.

Namur (50 29N 4 51E). Provincial capital with ancient citadel overlooking junction of Meuse and Sambre rivers. Industries include cutlery, glass, tanning and flour-milling. Pop. 32,000.

Nieuwepoort (51 8N 2 45E). Fishing port at mouth of R. Yser. Yachting harbour. Belgian troops maintained footing in area in World War I, by flooding German trenches.

Ostend (51 13N 3 0E). Principal Belgian fishing port. Important cross-Channel terminal. Harbour for yachts and general shipping. Important holiday resort, with many modern shops, casino and racecourse. Pop. 72,000.

Oudenarde (50 51N 3 37E). Industrial town. Brewing, textiles, especially linen and cotton. Scene of battle in which Marlborough defeated the French, 1708.

Roeselare (50 57N 3 08E). Important textile factories making linen, lace and carpets. Centre of the market-gardening, horticulture and orchard cultivation in area. Pop. 40,000.

Ronse (50 45N 3 36E). Textile town. Mainly engaged in weaving cotton and wool and manufacture of rayon, but also makes cheap cotton, woollen and linen goods. Pop. 25,000.

St. Hubert (50 2N 5 21E). Ardennes resort. Church containing the tomb of St. Hubert, patron saint of hunters. Has become a place of pilgrimage.

Saint Niklaas (51 10N 4 09E). Cotton-weaving town, but also manufactures rayon, carpets and hosiery. Market centre of the Waasland, a highly productive agricultural area reclaimed from the sea. Pop. 49,000.

Spa (50 29N 5 51E). Tourist centre in the Ardennes. Famous for its mineral springs. Has given its name to similar spa towns.

Tienen (50 49N 4 56E). Small industrial and market town. Trade in beer, grain, wool and cattle. Cotton and wool spinning. Best known for its beet-sugar refinery.

Tournai (50 37N 3 23E). Ancient industrial town on R. Scheldt. Manufactures carpets, hosiery, cement and leather goods. First Belgian town to be liberated by British troops in World War II. Pop. 33,000.

Turnhout (51 21N 4 47E). Well-known for linen-weaving and especially for its fine lace. Canvas and cotton goods also manufactured. Printing includes manufacture of playing cards. Town Hall was once a palace of the Dukes of Brabant. Pop. 38,000.

Verviers (50 36N 5 52E). Eastern and western ends of town almost entirely industrial. Produces large part of Belgium's woollen goods. Making of gingerbread is a speciality, and there is also a chocolate works. Pop. 32,000.

Veurne (51 5N 2 40E). Flanders town, famous for its Procession of the Penitents. Headquarters town during the Spanish occupation. Now only important as a communications centre.

Waterloo (50 45N 4 22E). 17 km (12 miles) south of Brussels. Scene of battle in which Wellington and Blücher defeated French under Napoleon, 1815.

Ypres (50 52N 2 52E). One of the great centres of the medieval cloth trade. Modern industries include engineering and food manufacturing. Tobacco is grown in the district. Scene of three great battles in World War I. Town later rebuilt and ancient buildings recreated.

Index

BELGIUM and LUXEMBOURG
Physical

Cities and Towns

International Boundaries

Mountain Peaks (in feet)   ▲ 1837

Points Below Sea Level   ▼ -12

feet	metres
1000	366
500	183
0	0

Below Sea Level

Scale 1:1,250,000

Projection: Conical